A North Wall Production

Fast Track

by Catriona Kerridge

Published by Playdead Press 2014

A CIP catalogue record for this book is available from the British Library.

ISBN 978-1-910067-25-3

Printed by CMP-UK

Playdead Press
www.playdeadpress.com

FAST TRACK
written by Catriona Kerridge

A North Wall production.

First performed at The North Wall Arts Centre, October 2nd
– 4th 2014

The Cast

Elaina	Emma Dennis-Edwards
Lucia	Fumilayo Brown-Olateju
Sax	Archie Rush
Tom	Christopher Finnegan
Anna	Ailsa Joy
Josh	Matthew Milner

The Creative Team

Director	Lucy Maycock
Designer	Alex Berry
Design Assistant	Chloe Dunscombe
Music composed and performed by	Carlos Posada and Jamie Jay
Lighting Design	Alexandra Faye Braithwaite
Production Manager	Clive Stevenson
Stage Manager	Hayley Constable

Many thanks to:

St Edward's Oxford, without whose ongoing generous support none of this could happen

The Arts Council of England

The Garfield Weston Foundation

High Tide Festival Theatre

Oxford Playhouse

Fumilayo Brown-Olateju | Lucia

Fumilayo has just graduated from the University of Kent. She decided to reignite her passion for acting and get back into the business after a 4 year hiatus while studying. While auditioning for the North Wall Summer Outreach programme she was selected by director Lucy Maycock to join the cast of Fast Track. Her previous credits include: *The Beggars Opera* (Stage), *ROOTS: Child Soldiers* (Stage), WII Sports Commercial & an NHS Billboard Ad Campaign

Emma Dennis-Edwards | Elaina

Emma trained at East 15 Acting School. Theatre credits include: *Clean* (Traverse Theatre, 59e59 Theaters, New York), *Millennium* (The Vineyard Theatre, New York), *Hurried Steps* (The Finborough Theatre, The Cockpit Theatre, Dukes Theatre, Lancaster), *Crash* (The North Wall Arts Centre and Arcola Theatre), *Talent* (Soho Theatre), *Upper Cut* (TARA Arts), *The Roaring Girl* (Shakespeare's Globe), *A New World Order* (The Barbican and Shoreditch Town Hall), *Bussin' It* (Ovalhouse Theatre and Camp Bestival). Television and film credits include: *Over the Rainbow* (BBC Ident), *Trap for Cinderella* (Forthcoming Productions) and *The Naked Poet* (Triple Threat Media).

Christopher Finnegan | Tom

Christopher Finnegan trained at Manchester Metropolitan School of Theatre. Theatre credits while training include *A Midsummer Night's Dream, Henry VI part 1, Henry VI parts 1 & 3,* and *King Lear.* Christopher has also been heavily involved with The North Wall's work over the past two years, where his credits include *Riot* (2013) and *Crash* (2012). He is also currently working on *Song of Riots* (Awake Projects / The North Wall), scheduled to tour in 2015.

Ailsa Joy | Anna

Ailsa Joy trained at RADA. Her theatre credits include: *The Wind in the Willows* (Polka Theatre), *Much Ado about Nothing, The Arabian Nights, Pride and Prejudice* (Drill Hall), *The Crucible* (Oxford Playhouse), *The Siren's Call* (Watermill Theatre), *Seeing Things* (Shakespeare Week), *Cake, 'Tis Pity She's a Whore, Peer Gynt* (The North Wall). Audio credits include: *Skybreaker* (Full Cast Audio), *The Middle of Nowhere* (Oakhill), *The Positively Last Performance* (AudioGo), *Bellerophon and Pegasus* (The Story Museum.) Theatre whilst training includes: *The House of Special Purpose, Twelfth Night, The Maids, Divine Words* and *Cymbeline.*

Matthew Milner | Josh

Matthew is currently studying at UCL. Theatre credits include: *Crash*, *Having a Ball* (The North Wall), *Together* (Arcola Theatre), *1984* (The Bloomsbury Theatre), *Little Pieces of Love* (Southwark Playhouse), *The Challenging Tide* (Theatro Technis), *One Flew Over The Cuckoo's Nest* (EmpathEyes), *Melting Bridges and Falling Snow*, *The Melting Point* (Iodine Teater). He is an associate artist of the Awake Projects.

Archie Rush | Sax

Fast Track is Archie's professional stage debut and he is very excited to be joining the company at The North Wall. Archie is a member of the National Youth Theatre, and previous theatre includes *Macbeth* (Youth Music Theatre UK, Berkshire), and roles as Gregor in *Metamorphosis*, Jim in *Chatroom*, Eric in *Lord of the Flies*, Doody in *Grease* at the Bedford School Theatre.

Film Credits include a project by artist Andy Holden, presented as a multimedia installation at the Zabludowicz collection, exhibited initially in London and now in Bristol.

Catriona Kerridge | Writer

Catriona was born and grew up in Oxford, studied at Birmingham University, and then went on to complete an MA in Advanced Theatre Practice at the Royal Central School of Speech and Drama. Catriona is an alumnus of the Royal Court Young Writers Programme, and also the North Wall's Outreach programme, and has been supported by the North Wall, High Tide Festival Theatre and the Arts Council.

Working both collaboratively and independently. Catriona has written for: Paines Plough and the Oxford Playhouse (*Come to where I'm from*), National Theatre Studio (*Aftershocks London*), Salt Theatre (*Write at the heart: 1*). She recently won a writing competition for Time Zone Theatre and the Austrian Culture Forum, with a production currently in rehearsal at London's Tristan Bates Theatre. Catriona is also co-founder and writer for Bad Host Theatre, who have performed at the Bush theatre, Shambala music festival, Factory Junction, Old Fire Station and BAC. Catriona has recently worked for the international theatre company In Transit, and is also a published poet (Mardibooks: *The Dance is New*). October 2014 is a busy month for Catriona, with the performance of *Fast Track* at the North Wall, plus *SWINES* (a Bad Host production) at 47/49 Tanner Street, *Shoot, I didn't mean that* (Time Zone Theatre) at the Tristan Bates Theatre and a Paines Plough collaboration at the South Bank Centre Literary Festival.

Lucy Maycock | Director

Lucy Maycock has worked extensively as an actor, writer, director and teacher both here and in the USA. She was heavily involved in the setting up of the North Wall Arts Centre and has been its Artistic Director since 2010. She has co-directed most of the North Wall's production projects with young artists, and is currently associate writer/director with the Awake Projects, an international ensemble company based in Sweden.

Alex Berry | Designer

Alex Berry trained at the Royal Northern College of Music, and performed throughout the UK and Europe before pursuing a new career in theatre design. She is a recent graduate of the Bristol Old Vic Theatre Design MA course. Alex first came to The North Wall through their Outreach Project in 2011 and has since built up a strong relationship with the theatre, designing their in-house production *Dead On Her Feet* by Ron Hutchinson which toured to the Arcola Theatre in October 2012. Her recent credits include *Blue Stockings* (Tobacco Factory), *The River* (Brewery Theatre), *Peter and the Wolf (and Me)* (Bristol Old Vic Studio), *The Merry Wives of Windsor* (Redgrave Theatre), *Awake* (Edinburgh Fringe, C Venues) and TedX EastEnd (Stratford Circus). Future projects include *Song of Riots (Awake Projects / North Wall)*, and Ilana Turner's *O Réjane* at The Bootleg Theatre, Los Angeles in November 2014. www.alexberry.co.uk

Carlos Posada | Co-Composer

Carlos recently graduated from Pembroke College, Oxford. He now works as a freelance composer, and is the guitarist and keyboardist of the band Wild Swim, whose early singles were received favourably by publications including the Guardian, the Saturday and Sunday Times, NME and Clash magazine, and who will be looking to release more music early next year. Carlos has collaborated with Lucy Maycock on a number of productions before including *Henry V, Our Country's Good* and *Romeo and Juliet*, although this will be the first time that he and co-composer Jamie Jay will have written an entire original score for a theatrical production.

Jamie Jay | Co-Composer

Jamie is an Oxfordshire-based musician and composer. Starting out as a classical 'cellist, he now pursues a wide range of contemporary projects. He recently graduated from Leeds University, where he specialized in new music composition and contemporary philosophy and aesthetics. At Leeds he completed a dissertation evaluating the music software Ableton Live, which is used throughout the performance of *Fast Track*. He has written scores for theatre productions and short films. He also writes, performs and produces in the band Wild Swim, and under various electronic guises.

Alexandra Faye Braithwaite | Lighting Designer

Alex trained at LAMDA. Recent designs include: *'The Wind In The Willows'* The North Wall Arts Centre; *'Grumpy Old Women III'* UK Tour; *'Olives & Blood'* Brixton East; *'The Fastest Clock In The Universe'* Old Red Lion Theatre; *'But Not As We Know It'* London Academy Of Music & Dramatic Art; *'XY'* Theatre 503 & Pleasance Courtyard, Edinburgh; *'Can't Stand Up For Falling Down'* The White Bear Theatre; *'The Shelter'* Riverside Studios; *'Project Strip'* Tara Arts; *'Lonely Soldiers: Woman at War in Iraq'* Brixton East & Arts Theatre; *'The Dreamer Examines His Pillow'* Old Red Lion Theatre; *'Useless'* Brixton East; *'Faustus'* The Old Laundry Theatre; *'Blackout'* Castle Theatre. And as Associate: *'Secret Theatre Show 4'* The Lyric Hammersmith; *'Jumpers For Goalposts'* Paines Plough / Watford Palace & Hull Truck.

THE NORTH WALL ARTS CENTRE AND TRUST

The North Wall exists to provide opportunities for artists, young people and the general public to make and experience art of the highest quality. We aim to promote the notion of art as a tool for living; timely, relevant and socially engaged. Through the cutting-edge programming choices of the Arts Centre and ground-breaking outreach initiatives for aspiring young artists, we aim to offer both cultural enrichment for audiences, and an 'arts laboratory': a place where people of different ages, experience and disciplines can come together, make connections and explore new ideas and aesthetics. We have a focus on nurturing talent in young and emerging artists, and removing the barriers that prevent them from achieving meaningful careers in the arts. The North Wall Trust, established in 2012, provides a platform for this work, managing a range of home-grown artistic outputs, including vocational training and outreach projects, productions, co-productions and a range of participatory and educational initiatives for young people and the wider community.

The North Wall Arts Centre
South Parade
Oxford
OX2 7JN

Box Office: 01865 319450 | Email: contact@thenorthwall.com

***Fast Track* and the North Wall Outreach Programme**

Since 2007, the North Wall has become known for running highly successful residential projects that bring established practitioners together with young artists aged 18-25 in an intensive theatre-making laboratory – with transformative results for all who take part. Skilled project directors /facilitators spend 3 weeks living and working with 20-30 talented young performers, writers, designers, musicians and technicians, who receive the entire experience free of charge. The resulting synergies have been inspirational: changing lives, forming new networks, and creating work of exceptional quality.

Fast Track began its life during just such a project in the summer of 2012. To complement the North Wall's first ever foray into full-scale producing: (a piece about recession, but seen through the historical lens of America's Great Depression), the Outreach project asked the young artists involved to create a more contemporary response to economic crisis. *Fast Track* received rehearsed readings at that time in both the North Wall and London's Arcola Theatre, and was then nurtured and developed both at the North Wall and through High Tide's Escalator programme, and Catriona Kerridge received Arts Council support to develop the project.

Two years in the making, The North Wall is delighted to now be able to see the project through to fruition, and give this exciting new script the full staging it deserves.

For The North Wall:

Lucy Maycock	(Artistic Director)
Sherrell Perkin	(General Manager)
Clive Stevenson	(Technical Manager)
Amy Walters	(Theatre and Marketing Manager)
Hayley Constable	(Technician / Stage Manager)
Alexandra Braithwaite	(Theatre Technician / Lighting and Sound Designer)
Niamh Watson	(Box Office / FOH Assistant)

Fast Track

Josh	Thirties
Anna	Late twenties
Elaina	Sixteen
Lucia	Fifteen
Sax	Fourteen
Tom	Twenty Two

'Every city has a park, every town has a park, and you will spend most of your youth there.'

"I was walking in the park and this guy waved at me. Then he said, 'I'm sorry, I thought you were someone else.' I said, 'I am.'"

Demitri Marti

"The Hunchback in the Park...
All night in the unmade park
After the railings and shrubberies
The birds the grass the trees the lake
And the wild boys innocent as strawberries
Had followed the hunchback
To his kennel in the dark."

Dylan Thomas.

Josh is standing on a bench. He looks up at the sky and smiles. Like a conductor he opens his arms to the sky and breathes in heavily. He is wearing his shirt, boxers and socks. He sits down and takes his socks off and carefully folds them and places them on a pile of clothes next to him. He sits.

In the Flat: Sax is seen counting 1ps and 2ps. Once he counts up enough he pops the money in to little plastic bags. Tom is playing football by himself banging the ball against the wall rhythmically.

Elaina and Lucia are listening to music – sunbathing and chilling/hanging out. They are dressed for summer.

Anna is wearing her jogging kit. She is sorting out her earphones, looping them under her top. She takes a swig of water. Presses play on her Ipod: music starts playing loudly. She runs around the audience, doing laps.

Scene 1: '*Day Fifteen*'

The park. Music is playing and Elaina is humming along occasionally…

Elaina: Right. This is it.

Lucia: What?

Elaina: Day Fifteen.

Lucia: Of what?

Elaina: Summer.

Lucia: Is that good or bad?

Elaina: It's like a Wednesday. Right in the middle and a bit frustrating.

Lucia: Got us a tenner.

Elaina: A tenner won't get us anything.

Lucia: And what have you got us?

Elaina puts her hand in her pocket and then holds it clasped closed.

Elaina: Look -

Lucia looks at her hand.

Lucia: You got us money?

Elaina: No. *She slaps her 'lightly' in the face.* I got you a slap in the face. Been working on it for weeks.

Lucia rubs her cheek.

Lucia: So all we've got is a tenner. Shall we make a list?

Elaina: Whatever.

Scene 2: '*Brothers care*'

There is a young boy on stage: Sax. He has a huge glass bottle full of pennies, 2p's and 1p's. And he is carefully counting them and putting them into little plastic bags.

Sax: *(singing)* 'It's all about the money-money-money.'

Tom: That's not how the song goes.

Sax: So.

Tom: It's not about the money, that's what she says.

Sax: Almost on to ten pounds here.

Tom: Shit you're rich. Filthy rich.

Sax: *(Smiles)* Yeah. *(continues counting)* 77-78-79-80-81...*(cont.)/*

Tom: /10 15 46 108 19 12

Sax: Stop it I can't concentrate.

Tom: 21 24 89 66 1234

Tom swipes his head.

Sax: What was that for?

Tom: Go have your shower.

Sax: You're not my Mum. *Beat.* Just gotta finish this bag.

19

Sax puts the final coins in. Tom takes a bag and examines it.

Tom: How much is that then?

Sax: A pound.

Tom: That's a pound?

Sax: Yeah.

Tom: It smells in here.

Sax smells his own armpit and smiles satisfied.

Sax: The smell of success.

Tom: The smell of success will be when you remember to put deodorant on.

Sax: You wait. I'm going to be an entrepioneer.

Tom: An entrepreneur.

Sax: Whatever. You wait. I'll be hired and you'll be fired.

Sax gets out the next lot of coins from his glass bottle.

Tom: You're a loser. You know that right? A spotty, sweaty little squirt. Now go have your shower?

Sax: Don't want to and don't have to.

Tom: Stop being a teenager.

Sax: I am a teenager.

Tom picks up five bags of money.

Get off my money. That's mine.

Tom: No it's not – most of it's from my room isn't it? I leave it lying on the side, the shitty coins and then they're gone. So this is mine – all of it.

Sax: You chuck 'em in the bin.

Tom: I can do what I want with my money.

Sax: You just waste it all. Fucking waster.

Tom: What did you say?

Sax: Waster.

Tom: You shouldn't talk to me like that. And all that swearing.

Sax: I'm not a kid anymore. You can't tell me what to do or what to say. – I can say what the fuck I like. And say what I want when I want. So wait – erm – Fuck – Twat – Wanka – Arsehole – Fuck – Twat – Wanka – Arsehole (...)

Tom takes him in a headlock and grabs a bag of coins.

Tom: Right. Open your mouth. I'll shove one of your pounds straight in to that swear box of yours. Go on, eat it. Say ahhh-

Sax shuts his mouth tightly. Tom tries to shove the bag of coins in to Sax's mouth.

Sax: *(with his mouth shut)* Stop it. Don't.

Eventually Tom lets go of Sax.

Tom: Just be nice yeah. Go have a shower. Stop swearing and ask me next time, ask me before you help yourself yeah? I'm trying to teach you some manners.

Sax: What manners? Never seen any of those around?

Tom: Stop it.

Sax: Sorry.

There's a knock on the door. Sax is about to get up and Tom pushes him back down.

Tom: I'll get it.

As soon as Tom leaves the room Sax starts going through Tom's stuff. – Football kit bag. He finds the wallet and looks through it. He finds a £10 note and stuffs it into his pocket.

Sax: *(shouts)* What's for dinner?

There is a knock on the door again. Sax continues singing and counting.

<u>Scene 3:</u> *'Friendship Test'*

Elaina, Lucia and Anna.

Elaina and Lucia are writing a list. Elaina is fidgety looking at her phone.

Lucia: Strawberries.

Elaina: Ice cubes.

Lucia: Chocolate.

Elaina: Fuck the chocolate what about the cider?

Lucia: I'm not buying ice cubes.

Elaina takes the pen.

Elaina: We don't need strawberries.

Lucia: All right then just cider.

Elaina: Perfect.

They watch Anna jogging past.

Lucia: Why do people do that?

Elaina: What?

Lucia: Jog?

Elaina: Maybe she's single.

Lucia: What you go on a jog to meet someone?

Elaina: No but –

23

Lucia:	Everyone's doing it –
Elaina:	I'm not.
Lucia:	I know but everyone else is.
Elaina:	Do you want to?
Lucia:	No- Do you think she earns a lot?
Elaina:	Probably loaded.
Lucia:	How much.
Elaina:	Thirty to forty grand.
Lucia:	What do you think she does? – it's three o'clock.
Elaina:	She looks like a doctor.
Lucia:	A dentist.
Elaina:	Nah – doesn't look like a dentist. She's a /
Lucia:	I bet she's a solicitor.
Elaina:	No wait she's – I've got it

Anna stops jogging, you can hear her music's still playing, she measures her heart rate and stretches. She continues doing this to her music.

	- she's a zoologist.
Lucia:	A zoologist?
Elaina:	Yeah –

Lucia: Go on then.

Elaina: What?

Lucia: Ask her.

Elaina: Ask her if she likes animals? - No way.

Lucia: I think you're wrong.

Elaina: No she looks like a Zoologist, I'm serious.

Lucia: Why would she not be at the zoo then?

Elaina: It's hot –

Lucia: And?

Elaina: And the animals are asleep.

Lucia: Whatever.

Elaina: Alright – Alright I'll ask her -

Lucia: Wait. So the rules are. You have to ask her if she's a zoologist. And you'll get triple points for touching her right foot. You have to use the word 'hot', and you have to use the word 'fuck'. And you have to ask her if she loves animals. And the camera will be the evidence.

Elaina: What's the prize this time?

Lucia: If you get all the points I'll give you this.

Takes out the note.

                        This tenner.

Elaina: Yeah?

Lucia: Yeah.

They shake hands and Elaina goes over to Anna. And looks to Lucia. Lucia gets her phone out and starts filming and turns their music off and give Elaina a thumbs up.

Elaina: Er... Yeah. Hi. My friend. She. Well I want
                     to ask you do you like animals?

Anna ignores Elaina and continues to listen to her music.

Elaina: Are you an animal lover? Do you love
                     them? Do you – do work at the zoo – where
                     is the zoo – is it far you know you look like
                     a zoologist. I've never seen one but you look
                     hot. All that jogging. Oh, er.

Elaina touches Anna's right foot. Anna takes her headphones off.

                     Fuck –

Anna: What?

Elaina: Animals.

Anna: What?

Elaina: Do you... fuck - do you like animals?

Anna: What – Do I fuck animals?

Elaina: No. I meant –

Anna: You think that's funny?

She looks at Lucia.

                   Tell your friend to turn that thing off –

Elaina: So you don't work with animals?

Anna: No.

Elaina: But, we just wanted to know. What do you
                   do, do you work? it's 3'oclock. And/

Anna: I work with kids alright.

Elaina: Sorry – fuck – sorry I –

Anna: You want to ask me if I fuck kids, now.
                   Well the answer is no.

Elaina looks embarrassed and then looks over to Lucia.

                   What do you do?

Elaina: Nothing.

Anna: Well you should stick to what you're good
                   at.

Elaina: What?

Anna: Nothing.

*Anna puts her headphones on and starts running again to her
track 'This is what it feels like' or something similar. Lucia
starts slow clapping.*

Lucia: This is gold.

Elaina: It's embarrassing.

Lucia holds the phone toward Elaina.

Lucia: So was she a Zoologist?

Elaina: No.

Lucia: What does she do then?

Elaina: Turn it off.

Lucia: Want to know your score.

Elaina: Hand it over.

Lucia: No way, you cheated – she had headphones on – And you didn't touch her right foot.

Elaina: I did.

Lucia: Firstly you were aiming for her left foot.

You don't get special points for being dyslexic.

Elaina: I touched her right foot.

Lucia: Secondly you didn't touch it. You know what the word touch means right? You poked it. *She holds her phone out to Elaina.* Wanna see?

Lucia pokes Elaina. Elaina swipes her away.

Elaina: Fuck sake.

Lucia: Come on-

Elaina: Stupid game. Made me look stupid.

Lucia: Alright – We can always have a re-match if that's what you want.

Elaina: Whatever. What are we doing?

Lucia: Nothing.

Elaina: Fuck it – let's get the cider.

They start walking.

   And then it's your turn.

(Whilst they exit Elaina pushes her)

Lucia: Stop it.

Push

Elaina: Get off.

<u>Scene 4.</u> *'A breath of fresh air'*

Tom spraying Sax with Febreze.

Sax: Get off me. What you doing?

Tom: You gave me no choice. At least now you're as fresh as

He reads the label.

          As fresh as a blossom breeze.

Tom sits down with his hand on his face.

          Now go – go outside.

Sax stands and stares at him.

          What?

Sax: Who was at the door?

Tom: Just some charity.

Sax: Right.

Tom: What?

Sax: You didn't answer the door.

Tom: So.

Sax: How do you know what they wanted?

Tom: I looked through the peep hole and saw a tall man and a short woman wearing black coats and holding red books. They may as well have had Jesus hanging out on a cross with them. That's how obvious it was. Now – go and get out.

Sax: What's for dinner?

Tom: Coco-pops.

Sax: And milk?

Tom: No. I'm gonna spit on them instead.

Sax: Just asking. Cos the milks gone off. Think the fridge is broken.

Tom: What do you mean?

Sax: Yeah and the light don't work –

Tom: Just go will you. *(He looks at the bags of money)* And take that shit with you.

Sax puts them in his bag and goes to his trolley.

Sax: Wanna come sell rides with me?

Tom: No.

Sax: It'll be fun.

Tom: Wanna do some cleaning?

Sax: Will you pay me?

Tom: No. So you wanna do some tidying?

Sax: No.

31

Tom: Thought not. Now go.

Sax looks at Tom.

What?

Thought you weren't a kid anymore.

Sax: Please.

Tom: Alright. If Zombies attack.

Sax: We will fight.

Tom: When we sink into the ocean.

Sax: We will swim.

Tom: Before time there was man.

Sax: And before man there were two brothers.

They salute each other. Tom sits on the sofa. Sax exits singing 'it's all about the money – money – money'.

Tom: Piss off.

<u>Scene 5. 'Baby face'</u>

In the park the girls have just been kicked out of a shop.

Elaina: *(shouting back to where they have just come from)* You know what - Fuck you!/

Lucia: /Run. /

Elaina: /Don't wanna give you any of my money anyway. Treating customers like that. You fucking racist shits-

Lucia: Maybe we should just get strawberries.

Elaina: It's your fault.

Lucia: What?

Elaina: Baby face.

Lucia: That's not fair.

Elaina: You've got a baby face. No, wait, you look like you're 12.

Lucia: Harsh.

Elaina: The truth hurts.

Lucia: Let's just go to the next shop.

Elaina: Have you even hit puberty? Babyface.

Lucia: I don't have a baby face.

Elaina: Prove it.

Lucia:	Alright. You know what. I'll go to the next shop.

Lucia starts walking. Elaina starts following.

Elaina:	I wanna see this. I'll wait outside.
Lucia:	No. Wait here.
Elaina:	And what am I gonna do?
Lucia:	Wait.
Elaina:	I don't like waiting.
Lucia:	Do you want cider or not?
Elaina:	Fuck it. I don't even like cider.
Lucia:	You don't like cider?
Elaina:	No.
Lucia:	Why did you put it on the list then?
Elaina:	What list?
Lucia:	Why do you want us to drink it?
Elaina:	I don't.
Lucia:	You piss me off sometimes.
Elaina:	Cider's boring.
Lucia:	You know what. I don't have a baby face. Your fake ID looks fake. That's what's wrong.

Elaina:	It doesn't. It's real.
Lucia:	Let's see.
	Where did you get it?
Elaina:	I er-
Lucia:	You nicked it didn't you.

Elaina takes it out of her hand.

Elaina:	Can't exactly take my mum's can I?
Lucia:	You don't even have the same eye colour.
Elaina:	Got coloured contact lenses on.
Lucia:	What about the nose?
Elaina:	That's the angle. *(She tilts her head)* See?
Lucia:	To get a nose like that you'll need a nose job. Slice off about an inch.
Elaina:	Alright – it doesn't look like me. But it's all in the confidence of the way you do it. Hand it over – make them feel embarrassed about asking. And then –
Lucia:	Bullshit.
Elaina:	Don't get the cider.
Lucia:	What do you want?
Elaina:	Bacardi.

Lucia:	And coke?
Elaina:	Just Bacardi.
Lucia:	Alright.
Elaina:	And if you can't get it. We can just buy some mouthwash.
Lucia:	What?
Elaina:	Yeah – you can get it with alcohol in it. The worst it will do – is make your breath smell better.
Lucia:	Are you joking?
Elaina:	About your breath stinking or the drinking?
Lucia:	You can't be serious.
Elaina:	Go on.
Lucia:	Right – Bacardi – I'll get the Bacardi with my money.
Elaina:	Yeah and then it's your turn next. I need to film you. I've got an idea.

(knock cue x 3 – which makes all the others respond – Tom (muttering): Go away, go away…)

<u>Scene 6: *'Strange-strangers'.*</u>

Anna stops running and starts scratching her head frantically. She then starts shaking her body and groaning. She's listening to her ipod. Josh is hiding under the bench. Josh is only wearing a shirt and boxer shorts. Anna sits on the bench. She takes out a half smoked cigarette and lights it. Anna removes her headphones. She drops the ash through the gaps and stubs it out on the bench. Letting it fall on to Josh. (As Anna is groaning she can say: go away go away – stop itching – fuck off.)

(Knock cue - Tom responds: go away, go away)

Josh: Please don't be alarmed. But there is a man under the bench.

She jumps up from the bench.

Anna: What?

She sees Josh lying under the bench. He emerges just with his torso.

Josh: Did you know it can take up to ten years for a cigarette filter to biodegrade?

Anna: What the fuck.

Josh: I know shocking.

Anna: I'm calling the police.

Josh: This isn't what it looks like.

Anna: Isn't it?

37

Josh: Well the thing is – you caught me at an awkward time here.

Anna: I can see that.

Josh: You see- its quite simple. I needed to dry my suit. And then I saw you coming. And I didn't want to scare you. I'm coming out.

Anna: What?

He wriggles his way out.

Josh: Nice day, isn't it? How long have we waited for a bit of vitamin D, eh? Been suffering too long. We're slipping into vitamin D deficiencies. It's a big concern you know.

Josh is stuck.

Erm – Yeah. I think I'm a bit stuck. I er- It's all gone tits up.

Anna picks up her bag and looks hesitantly at him and is ready to leave.

Please don't leave me like this. I have asthma. Can you at least – in my front pocket of the bag is my inhaler. It's a blue thing. Could you just pass it to me? You have to tug the zip a bit. It can be a bit dodgy.

Anna takes the bag and tries to open the front pocket.

You really have to yank it.

She finally gets his inhaler out. She passes it to Josh.

Josh takes a puff and holds his breath.

Anna: Are you okay?

He continues holding his breath.

Josh: Sorry, got to hold my breath so the stuff reaches my lungs otherwise it's a waste.

He manages to free himself from the bench. And wriggles out. He holds out his hand to Anna.

Josh: Hi I'm Josh.

Anna doesn't take his hand.

Anna: Hi.

Josh: Thank you. You probably think I'm a right weirdo.

Anna: Yes.

Josh: I guess this looks/

Anna: Odd.

Josh: It's nice – the sun – the fresh air. (*Josh points at a cloud.*) That one just there want to shoot it down, big fat grey cloud. Makes me want to write a letter of complaint or suggest we find a way to blow those buggers away.

Anna starts getting ready to set off again.

	Wait. Can I just ask you something?
Anna:	Yes.
Josh:	Are you a dancer?
Anna:	No.
Josh:	What was that dance thing just then?
Anna:	What dance?

Josh imitates her moves.

Anna:	Oh – god you saw that.
Josh:	Sorry – two left feet. Probably didn't do it justice.

Anna laughs and sits down.

Anna:	No it was great.
Josh:	Great. (*Josh shoots down a cloud*).
	Do you know why the great depression was called great? What's great about it?
Anna:	I don't know.
Josh:	And mortgage, a mortgage. The word mort means death and gage means pledge so why would I want that – a death pledge, sign myself off to the devil. Why would anyone want to do that?

Anna: In Italian the word for investor, investir can mean to invest and to collide with, to run over –

Josh: Do you speak Italian?

Anna: No.

She takes out another cigarette from her pocket and twists it around in her hand.

Josh: It's a nice spot isn't it?

Anna: Yes.

Josh: And the word philanthropist means humanitarian and to be a humanitarian you have to perform an act of giving.

Josh looks over at her cigarette. He passes her the cigarette butt from earlier. She takes it and chucks it behind her when he's not looking.

Is that a design thing?

Anna: What do you mean?

Josh: The line on your cigarette?

Anna: Oh no. That's just a thing.

Josh: *Josh pulls a packet of crisps out of his bag.*

Do you want some? *He holds out the packet to her.*

Salt and Vinegar.

41

Anna: No thanks.

Josh: Do you mind?

Anna: Go for it.

Josh eats some of the crisps. Anna twizzles her cigarette in her hand.

I'm trying to cut down. I mark them half way so I only smoke half. (*She takes the cigarette and shows him.*)

You might assume that this is half way but I worked it out with the filter, so I don't feel ripped off at the end. You know?

Josh: Go ahead. I don't mind.

Anna: Ten years?

Josh: Yeah. There are worse things. Plastic bag 10-20 years, plastic bottles 450 years. Nappies 550 years. Makes you wonder what archeologists will make of us.

Anna puts her cigarette back in her pocket. Anna takes her drink and realises it is empty. She sighs.

Josh: Thirsty?

Anna: I'm alright.

Anna puts the bottle down again. Josh is looking for something.

Josh: Run a lot?

Anna: Yeah. It's great. Everyone's doing it/

Josh: Coke?

Anna: Coke? No I mean jogging, everyone's jogging.

Josh lifts up a bag from behind the bench. He pulls out a couple of coke cans.

Josh: I found it. All wrapped up. Perfectly fine. Want one?

(*He struggles to open the plastic film.*)

I guess this is good – no rat shit or anything can get through this plastic wall of steel. One drink?

Anna: This is –

Josh: Unusual I know.

Anna: I can't-

Josh: One drink won't hurt. *He passes her a coke and she takes it.* A thank you for saving my life.

Anna: Alright.

They open it at the same time.

Were you hoping to meet someone?

They both drink.

Scene 7 *'Hi'*

Sax enters singing and dancing 'Sax machine' with his trolley that has been pimped up. Sax walks past Elaina with his shopping trolley. Elaina looks up at him. And laughs. Sax clocks her and tries to look 'cool' again.

Sax: Hi-

Elaina stays silent and looks at her hands.

Sax: Nice hands.

Elaina looks up.

Sax: Nice face.

Elaina starts walking away. Sax follows her with the trolley.

Sax: Nice hair-

Elaina stays silent.

Sax: Oh shit – you can't speak. Shit – that's got to be hard.

Elaina: Fuck off.

Sax: Want a ride?

Elaina: No –

Sax: Come on. It'll be fun.

Elaina: No way.

Sax: I do it for the old ladies mainly. Even got a little stepladder. Well my Stannah stair lift equivalent. Plastic crates.

Elaina smiles.

Elaina: You do it for old ladies?

Sax: Nah – well one, and then I do it for an old man. He loves a bit of a joy ride. I can go fast slow all sorts. It costs – well depends on distance but I'll give you a spin for 2 pounds.

Elaina: No way-

Sax: Alright. One. One pound.

Elaina shakes her head. Sax starts spinning the trolley from side to side. And then starts humming 'Price Tag'

Sax: All right – It's not about the money, money, money. When it comes to you. I'll do it for free but you have to advertise. Okay?

Elaina looks up.

Elaina: I'm not doing it.

Sax: Got anything else to do?

Elaina shrugs.

Sax: No loss then.

Elaina: I'm waiting for someone.

Sax: Boring.

Elaina: I don't know. How do I know it's safe?

Sax: Well I've put 20 potato bags in it before - that's like 25 kilograms times 20. How much do you weigh?

Elaina: Not telling.

Sax: More or less.

Elaina: Less.

Sax: So you weigh less than 500kg.

Elaina: I think you're bullshitting.

Sax: I swear on my brother's life I gave this old thing a good old test run.

Sax looks down then smiles at her. And waits.

Elaina: Alright.

Sax holds out his hand

Sax: Sax by the way. Good doing business with you.

Elaina: I'm not paying.

Sax: What's your name?

Elaina: Elaina

Sax: Once you've had this ride, Elaina. You will be my promo girl.

Elaina: I won't be a promo girl.

Sax: Well – whatever. You'll love it.

Elaina: You're talking me out of it.

Sax quickly gets the crate out and invites Elaina to stand on it. She gets on and steps in to the trolley. And he pushes her gently.

Elaina: Boring.

Sax: Alright here goes –

They skid around the audience.

Elaina: You need some speakers or something.

Sax starts beat boxing/singing.

Scene 8. '*I want don't have*'

Tom. Tom is in the flat looking out of the window.

Tom: Haven't got any speakers or expensive ipads.

I got a flat screen colour TV.

A load of Mum's cheap jewelry.

Three beds and a load of bed sheets.

Some frames with Unicorns on it.

I got a sofa with memories torn on to it.

A load of clothes that are really old and smell of mold.

Some of Plates with chips.

This Carpet with rips on it.

Gameboy colour that's sixteen bit.

And Mum's bottlenose dolphin that's missing its tip.

I can see you. I can see you sat out there in the car. Magpies. Filthy magpies. Look at you. Living the dream are you? Waiting for that moment where you can come up here and just take our shit. And it's all just shit. Means nothing to you. Just a load of stuff you might be able to flog. Piss off! You can't have any of it. I know my rights. You can knock as much as you like I'm not going to let you in. You can't gain access to this property without an invitation. No matter what you threaten me with. You're not having any of it. What? You want the sofa? (*Looks it up and down*) In pretty good nick could sell it for a few. But it's worth more than that. This sofa's got fucking memories. I had sex on that sofa. Well not on the sofa, behind the sofa. This sofa's been a boat, a submarine, a space ship and Santa's fucking sledge.

He looks at the Sofa.

And where Sax fell asleep and I super glued all the feathers to him. Made him believe that he was growing wings. And then the teacher spotted his skin. Sax had to go to hospital. And now what the fuck should we do? You want the sofa? The Fridge? Why don't you just take it all –Come on: Take it. Take the lot. Try and flog it. Come on look, look what we've got:

(starts dancing/impro/fake rapping)

I got a flat screen colour TV.

A load of Mum's cheap jewelry.

Three beds and a load of bed sheets.

Some frames with Unicorns on it.

I got a sofa with memories torn on to it.

A load of clothes that are really old and smell of mold.

Some of Plates with chips.

This Carpet with rips on it.

Gameboy colour that's sixteen bit.

And Mum's bottlenose dolphin that's missing its tip.

(As the song plays we see the trolley come in with Elaina screaming – they exit)

Tom carries on – a knock is heard. He stares –at the door.

Scene 9. '*Just having a dance*'

Anna and Josh in the park at the bench. Josh gets up to put the empty coke cans in the bin.

Anna: It's Anna.

Josh: So that dance?

Anna: Yep.

Josh: Looked tribal.

Anna: It's the kids.

Josh: How many?

Anna: Kids or Nits?

Josh: Kids.

Anna: Three.

Josh: Yours?

Anna: No. I do it for the cash.

Josh: Can I see one?

Anna: What a nit? Alright.

Josh heads over to have a look.

Josh: There-

Anna: *(lets out a sound)*

Anna shakes her head frantically and scratches. It looks like she's possessed.

Josh: It's okay.

Anna: Sorry.

Josh: Do you want me to get it out?

Anna: Sure.

Josh picks out a nit.

Anna: Hitler.

Josh: What?

Anna: If I kill them I like them to be named after dictators Idi Amin, Pol Pot. Stalin and who doesn't want to assassinate Hitler?

Josh: You're re-writing history.

Anna: I studied history. Can I ask you to do something?

It's a bit embarrassing. *(She reaches into her pocket)* Is it weird?

Josh: What?

She holds out a nit comb.

Anna: I've got a comb. A nit comb.

Josh: Perfect.

Josh takes the nit comb.

Anna: It's just really hard to see the back of my head.

Josh starts parting her hair and making her tilt her head forward. And starts combing her hair. As soon as Josh gets one he shows her.

Josh: Mugabe – Robert Mugabe.

Anna: Take that you little shit.

He continues.

Josh: This one's suicidal. Just walking on to your comb. Tiny aren't they?

Anna: Never seen a nit before?

Josh: My first time.

Anna: You don't have kids?

Josh: No. *He looks at the nit.* Now this one - This one bears a remarkable resemblance – to – Leopold the 2nd.

Anna: I haven't told anyone this before.

Josh: What?

Anna: Don't laugh.

Josh: I won't.

Anna: I er-. I knew I had them. Riddled. Oh god. You'll think I'm weird.

Josh: You already think I am.

Anna: It was perfect timing really. My ex was coming to London with his mates. For a stag do. He's Bulgarian. He's a shit. It's never gonna work. But when he called... asked me to be his tour-guide... Offered to pay... – knows I need the money. I was pissed off. The guts – but I did it. I came armed. Felt like a suicide bomber. My mission was to destroy them. I bought some cheap union jack hats. And for my X an 'I heart London' hoody, all covered with carefully placed itchy little bastards. I've got a photo of them all chanting Rule Britannia, with their proud union jack hats and him with his hood up. They loved it. Let him cuddle me, rub up against me. And then. In the middle of Trafalgar Square under Nelson and next to the Lions. I shouted. I just shouted: 'You're all shits! Fuck off back to your own country'. I don't know what came over me. But it felt good. Does that make me bad – evil – or worse, racist?

Josh: Ego te absolvo.

Anna: What did you say?

Josh: Latin for I absolve you. Used to work for the Church.

Anna: Catholic?

(cue for another knock)

Josh: Sometimes I am, sometimes I'm not.

(Knock)

Josh continues combing Anna's hair

<u>Scene 10. '*Falling apart*'</u>

The flat. There is a knock on the flat door. It repeats. Tom gets up and stares at the door.

Tom: Fuck off. I haven't got anything for you.

He goes to his wallet and looks inside,

Wanna see all I've got? (*He picks up the wallet*) All I've got is this Tenn-er – Fucksake – Could have sworn I had a tenner.

He picks up a cushion (song with the pre-recorded rap from previous scene) He feels the cushion that is stuffed with coins and tips it – he finds more and more.

He takes a moment and then takes it in – the obsession – the coins.

SAX!

<u>Scene 11</u>: *'Promo-girl'*

Elaina and Sax.

There's a loud scream. Elaina comes crashing through the audience. Sax runs up to the trolley and starts pulling it behind him. He then gives it a push and a pull and lets go. He makes it look like the trolley has knocked him to the ground.

Elaina: Shit-

Sax stays silent clutching his stomach. Elaina tries to get out of the trolley but is struggling. It keeps on moving.

Elaina: Are you alright?

Sax: Oh, Shit – it hurts. It's bad – really bad. Think I broke something. My stomach - gonna be sick. I can feel it. Wait – here it comes

        Got-Yah.

Elaina: That's not funny Dickhead.

He looks at Elaina and smiles. Then he grabs the trolley and starts pushing it again.

        Don't

Sax: It was only a stunt.

Elaina: I don't like it anymore.

Sax: Come on – you were laughing earlier.

Elaina: No I was screaming. Stop it.

Sax: You want to come out?

Elaina: Yeah.

He helps her step out of the trolley. He takes a blanket out of the shopping trolley and puts it over her shoulders.

Sax: It was fun though – right?

Elaina: Yeah was alright.

They sit on the crate.

Sax: Any feedback?

Sax writes some notes on a note pad.

Elaina: I like the – *(She smiles)* I like the design. I think you lack real music – And you need some more lights. Maybe brakes. Brakes would make me feel safer. Or wait – you could, well, you should really have a vom bag in there in case and – Will you drive me home later?

Sax: You want a ride?

Elaina: Yeah.

Sax: What time?

Elaina: You need to make cards – like a taxi. Can I have your number?

Sax: You want my number?

Elaina: Yeah.

Sax:	I can't.
Elaina:	You got a girlfriend or something?
Sax:	No. It's just.
Elaina:	Whatever.
Sax:	I don't have a phone.
Elaina:	You don't have a phone?
Sax:	No. I don't have a phone.

Elaina starts laughing.

What? What's so funny?

Elaina sits next to him and puts her arm around him.

Elaina: Shit, that's got to be hard. Really, hard. No wait. Are you from a different time? – does your trolley time travel? Are you a time traveler, from, from the 80s where mobiles didn't exist? Is that why you're trainers are so old?

Or wait are you like from the prehistoric times?

Sax gets upset

Sax: Stop it.

Just add me on facebook.

Elaina: Sorry. I was just having a laugh.

(Elaina looks at her phone and puts it away)

Lucia's tried calling me.

Sax: Who's she?

Elaina: My friend. She's just getting the booze.

Sax: You can call her back if you want-

Elaina: Nah I'm busy, right?

Sax: You want another ride?

Elaina: You're a bit of a loser aren't you?

Sax shrugs.

Sax: Still need a promo girl.

Elaina: I'm not a promo girl, I'm your partner.

Sax: Partner?

Elaina: Yeah business partner.

Sax: You serious?

Elaina: Yeah. I'll have to take a percentage.

Sax: How about some shares?

Elaina: Yeah.

Sax: How much?

Elaina: Shhh-

Elaina kisses him.

<u>Scene 12: '1-2-3-4-5- Once I caught a fish alive…'</u>

The flat has been turned over – Tom has found coins everywhere.
He steps back and stares at the coins.

Tom: How much? – How much is there? Each
bags a pound right? 1 -2 – 3 – 4 – 5 – 6 – 7 –
8 – 9 – 10 – 11 – 12 – 13- 14. – 15 – 16 – 17
– 18 – 19 – 20 – 21 – 22 – 23 – *(counting*
begins)

He then decides to count them. Putting them in neat piles –
ordering everything.

Scene 13. *'Confessing to a stranger'*

Anna and Josh are sitting on the bench. He is still looking through her hair.

Anna: How much?

Josh: What?

Anna: Well, do priests get paid?

Josh: Kind of. You get a pension plan, and basic support.

Anna: Sounds good – I'll have to die before I get a pension plan.

Josh: The root of all evil is money. And the problem is numbers, numbers are my thing – and there's nothing spiritual about that. Played with the church funds, rented out the parking spaces outside the church thought it made sense, empty most days. Invested the money, here and there. Gambled it, doubled it. Not really the path to heaven.

Take some – have a look.

Anna: What?

Josh: Getting rid of it all of it. Take it – Take what you want.

Anna: At least you've got stuff to give away. Now that is one good thing about my room. I can't accumulate stuff. My room is smaller than the baby's room. I can stand on my bed and touch both walls. Reckon the parents are scared to put the baby in my room in case its growth gets stunted. Like a goldfish.

(Josh pulls out the Rolex)

Found out yesterday that dog walkers get paid more than nannies. People value their dogs more than their kids.

Anna examines the watch.

Anna: Is that a Rolex?

Josh: Getting rid of it all of it.

Points at the Rolex.

From my finance days –

Anna: Finance.

Josh: Yes.

Anna: *(Anna pulls a phone out of the bag.)* There's an iphone in here.

Josh: Take it.

Anna: Why don't you give it all to Oxfam or something?

Josh: Yes, but the thing is there are just so many ways of doing it. Did you know, you can send stuff all across the world just from one place. I've got stuff going to Zanzibar, Mali, Togo, Timbuktu, Syria, Birmingham. A shirt went on Freecycle. My double-breasted stock cassock has been sent to a tiny village called Cadzand. I'm sending a hat to the Isle of Wight. Never met anyone from there. But he wanted my hat – and that's amazing.

Anna: You can post old phones back to the shop and they'll turn it in to cash.

Josh: I don't need cash.

Anna: Right.

Anna pulls out a photo.

Josh: Nick Drake.

Anna: That's Nick Drake – That's amazing.

Josh: It's an original. Keith Morris.

Anna: It's a nice photo.

Josh: Take it.

Anna: I can't.

Josh takes a pen from the bag. He writes on it.

Josh: There, wrote your name on it so you have to keep it. *(He spells out Anna)* A-N-N-A.

Anna: That's not how you spell Anna.

Josh: Really?

Anna: Just kidding.

Anna smiles.

Josh: There. A little forget me not.

He zips the picture up in to her bag.

Forget-me-nots grow all around here.

He sits back down next to her.

There's this story that when it came to God naming all things of the world, the little flower shouted 'forget-me-not' and to that God said: 'Well that shall be your name.'

Do you like Brighton?

Anna: I've never been.

Josh: I think you'd like the sea. Yes. Do you want any of the rest of this stuff?

Anna: Josh – that's your name right?

Josh: Yes.

Anna: Are you trying to convert me?

Josh: To what?

Anna: God.

Josh: Why?

Anna: Giving away all this stuff? Got to be something.

Josh: Not planning to convert you.

Anna: Are you – no – well are you – you know – thinking of –

Anna looks at the bag and looks back at him. She places her hand on his.

Josh: Suicide?

Anna: Are you?

Josh: Ah – No. Will you help me?

Anna: How?

Josh: Close your eyes – Please just close them. And wait here.

She hesitates.

Anna: What are you going to do?

Josh: I want to show you something.

He starts to undress.

Close your eyes, count to – 30.

Anna: 1 – 2 – 3 – 4 – 5 – 6 –

Josh exits.

Scene 14 'Count down'

Tom is counting.

Tom: 105-106-107-108-109-110-111-112-113-114-
115-116-117-118-119-120-121-22-23-24-25-
26-27-28-29-130-31-32-33-34-35-36-37-38-
39-40-41-2-3-4-5-6-7-8-9-50-1-2-3-4-5-6-7-
8-9-60—1-2-3-4-5-6-7-8-9-70-1-2-3-4-5-6-7-
8-9-70-1-2-3—4—5-6-7—8-9-80-1-2-3-4-5-
6-7-8-9 -90-1-2-3-4-5-6-7-8-99 100.

*(continues counting underscoring the next scenes till the ceiling
falls through)*

Scene 15 *'Rule Britannia'*

Elaina and Sax are still at their place kissing and giggling. Lucia arrives.

Lucia: Who's that?

Elaina: Our driver.

Sax: I should go.

Elaina grabs his hand.

Elaina: Don't.

Lucia: We don't need a driver.

Elaina: Trust me – we do.

Lucia throws her the blue plastic bag containing the mouthwash.

Lucia: Here.

Elaina: So you bailed.

Lucia: So, your breath stinks.

Elaina: Babyface.

Lucia: A tenner wasn't gonna get us anything.

Elaina: You got three.

Lucia: Special offer. Lucky really. I guess he'll want one too?

Sax: Nah I got to go, my brother/

Elaina: Come on

Sax: But/

Elaina: As your partner.

Lucia: Partner?

Elaina: Business.

Lucia: Right.

Elaina: I believe it's in your interest to drive us.

Lucia: He can't drive.

Elaina: Wait for it. It's awesome.

Sax: Alright.

Sax trumpet horns and gets a crate out of the trolley for the girls to step on to.

Lucia: You're not getting me in that thing.

Elaina: Yeah I am.

Lucia: It looks dangerous.

Elaina: Have you forgotten?

Lucia: What?

Elaina: It's your turn now. Can you spin this thing with both of us in it?

Sax: I can try.

Elaina: Lets drink and spin. Right. So this is the sitch. First up, get in the trolley will you. Come on Lucia don't be such a pussy.

Lucia gets in the trolley. Elaina joins her.

              Everybody bottles at the ready

Lucia: What?

Elaina: Can't you open the kiddy protection cap? Babyface.

Lucia opens her bottle.

Elaina: You too-

Sax: I don't need it.

Elaina: Trust me you do. It'll be more fun. After all, the right way to drive is to drink and drive.

Lucia: Drink and die.

Elaina: What you guys never drank mouth-wash before?

Elaina has a swig – and breathes out at Sax.

              Does my breath smell nice?

Sax: It's like that green shower gel-

Elaina: A boy told me once that, that stuff made his dick tingle.

Lucia: Shut up.

Sax: You want to spin right?

Elaina: Yeah!

Sax: Ready-

Elaina: Wait the rules are for every ready we all have to drink. And for every go *(to Lucia)* you have to stand up, with one hand on your heart and sing 'Rule Britannia' and salute anyone going past and – And I'll film it.

Sax: And sell some rides?

Elaina: Yeah.

Lucia: But/

Elaina holds her camera phone up.

Sax: Ready?

Bottles raised. They drink

           - Go.

Lucia stands up in the trolley on one leg. She salutes the audience and starts singing.

Lucia: Rule Britannia. Britannia rules the waves. I don't know the rest.

Elaina: Keep singing.

Lucia: Rule Britannia. Britannia rules the waves.

                    Da – da – dadadada- da –da – da .

They all join in.

                    Rule Britannia. Britannia rules the waves.

                    Da – da – dadadada- da –da – da

                    Rule Britannia. Britannia rules the waves.

                    Da – da – dadadada- da –da – da *(cont.)*...

Tom looks up. The ceiling is falling through. Coins everywhere!

Tom: Shit. Sax!

Lucia and Elaina scream as they hurtle through the audience

Second Half

The second half opens with the trolley passing – filled with stuff – Anna hesitating about staying or going…

Hide and seek.

Tom enters on bike – he cycles wearing a bag and then he shouts:

Tom: SAX.

He continues to cycle. He does this twice as he circles.

<u>Scene 1: *'Awesome'*</u>

Lucia and Elaina and Sax.

Lucia and Elaina giggle. Sax is pushing the trolley.

All singing: (*sings*) Only got twenty dollars in my pocket. This is fucking awesome. I wear my Grandad's clothes I look incredible...

STOP!

Sax stops the trolley. He offers the step to them but they just jump/climb out.

Elaina: Can't believe how much stuff people gave us. Just to get a ride.

Elaina takes a bottle and shakes it.

How about a minty wine cocktail?

Lucia: Give us a swig.

Lucia takes a swig.

Sax: Got so much stuff.

Lucia goes through all the stuff.

Elaina: Yeah. Thanks to your new promo girl *(Lucia)* and business partner. Got loads of good footage. It was amazing. That last guy with the white lightning, touched me up a bit *(She shrugs.)* But he gave us this.

She pulls a Swiss army knife from her pocket.

75

Sax:	What is it?
Elaina:	A Swiss army.
Lucia:	Knife. It's a swiss army knife.
Elaina:	It's not just a knife. It's got a corkscrew, a tooth pick, a nail file, some mini scissors. This isn't just a knife it's a fucking Swiss army knife.
Sax:	Right.
Elaina:	It's genuine. We could sell it on ebay, call it vintage.

Elaina examines it.

Sax:	What else did we get?
Lucia:	A t-shirt. Some olives. A bike pump, some half-drunk Cider, a hair tie, a bit of wine,
Elaina:	Half a spliff and a lighter.
Lucia:	A broken kite and a KFC bucket.

Lucia takes the spliff, Elaina lights it up for her. She takes a drag and passes it to

Elaina. Elaina takes a drag. Sax starts eating the chicken.

Sax:	Fuck a duck.
Elaina:	When female ducks have sex they get raped.

Lucia: Really?

Elaina: Yeah and because of that some of their vaginas have evolved to have pouches that dispose of unwanted sperm. And, some of them have a spiral inside them that goes the wrong way. So the male duck can't you know –

Lucia: What? Get its cock in?

Sax: That's disgusting.

Elaina passes Sax the spliff.

Elaina: Go on take it.

Sax: Nah, can't. My brother will kill me. Got a nose like a sniffer dog.

Lucia barks.

Elaina: Just febreze yourself afterwards.

Sax: No.

Lucia: I found this.

She holds out her hand a small plastic packet/or tablet. Sax looks at it.

Elaina: Let's see. He can't smell that can he?

Elaina passes the tablet to Sax.

                Go on *(To Sax)*

Lucia:	Don't think he wants to. He looks scared.
Elaina:	You only live once.
Sax:	I don't need it. I'm alright. I'm cool.
Lucia:	Never taken a tablet before?
Sax:	Yeah I have.
Elaina:	Go on then. Prove it.

Sax takes the packet. And hesitates.

Lucia:	This isn't paracetamol you know.
Sax:	I'm not stupid – you have it.
Lucia:	It's for you. A present.

Sax gets up to take it, he looks at them for a moment. Elaina waves the spliff at him

Elaina:	Us girls are sticking to this.

Sax swallows it and washes it down with the minty wine.

Lucia:	Got no idea what it is.
Elaina:	Me neither.

Lucia and Elaina giggle. Sax sits anxiously.

Lucia:	So. Spiral vaginas?
Elaina:	If they didn't have that we'd get over populated by ducks. There'd be ducks everywhere.

Lucia:	There would be a whole duck family in… …in your trolley-
Elaina:	On your hat.
Lucia:	On your face.
Elaina:	On your sofa watching telly.
Lucia:	In the club, in the pub.

The two girls laugh.

Elaina:	There would be ducks fucking everywhere.
Lucia:	Yeah. Fucking everywhere.
Sax:	Don't you have to go home?
Elaina:	Nah. We double bluffed. We were gonna go clubbing or something anyway. I told my parents that I was staying at Lucia's and Lucia did the opposite.
Sax:	It's getting dark. Won't you get in to trouble?
Elaina:	Mum says you shouldn't be here in the dark. She says: If you ever go to the park at night I won't feel sorry for you if you get raped. You'll have asked for it.
Sax:	Harsh.
Elaina:	Would you rape me Sax?
Sax:	I don't wanna rape anyone.

79

Elaina:	Yeah but if you had to rape someone who would it be?
	If you had to choose. Me or Lucia?
Lucia:	Don't.
Elaina:	It's alright. He'd choose me anyway.
Lucia:	But to be raped, you've got to not want it, right? So, you could never get raped. Because you're gagging for it. You would want it, so even if he hurt, it wouldn't be rape.
Elaina:	Inafuckingproopriate.
Lucia:	It's the truth.
Sax:	I love chicken.
Lucia:	Elaina doesn't like chicken.
Sax:	Who doesn't like chicken?
Lucia:	Vegetarians. She does it for weight-loss.
Elaina:	I don't, I just don't think it's okay to kill animals.
Lucia:	Hippy. Her family are hippies.
Elaina:	They're just trying to be trendy. Let's talk about Jesus. Now what do you think about him?
Lucia:	Don't.

Elaina starts waving at the sky.

	What you doing?
Elaina:	Waving. Saying hello to the big man.
Lucia:	Stop it.
Elaina:	Hello – God.
Lucia:	That's not fair.
Elaina:	You know Santa and the tooth fairy yeah?
Lucia:	Just stop it.
Elaina:	There's just so many – that's the problem – so many Gods – too much choice –

She drinks.

	So, if there is a God. What do you think will happen to me – I'm not baptized where will I go?
Lucia:	I don't know.
Elaina:	Will I go to hell?
Lucia:	No.
Elaina:	Well what do you think?
Lucia:	I don't know. Remember asking Dad where Jesus was. And he said he was everywhere. We were in my bedroom so I asked Dad if he was in the bed with us or sat in the room

81

watching. And he said yes. So I said. Can you ask him to go away please, to leave us alone.

Elaina: Was your Dad in bed with you?

Lucia gives Elaina a 'fuck you look'. Sax continues eating chicken.

Sax: I just hate him.

Lucia: Have you met him?

Elaina: He's not talking about Jesus or your Dad. Probs means his brother.

She kisses him on the cheek.

Hate means love.

Lucia: No it doesn't.

Elaina: If you're willing to go through the effort of hating someone then that means you actually love them. It's a love hate kind of thing. Don't worry Sax. You're in trouble aren't you? Everyone's in trouble. It's like the whole world is in trouble.

Lucia: I'm not in trouble.

Elaina: Apart from Lucia. She's never in trouble because she's a lonely only child.

Lucia: I'm not a lonely or an only child.

Elaina: Shit forgot about your brother.

Lucia: You're just shit stirring.

Sax: How old's your brother?

Elaina: (*She lowers her voice*) He's disabled.

Lucia: That doesn't mean he doesn't age. He's twenty-two.

Sax: Mines 22.

Elaina: Is yours disabled too? Because right now it looks like you two have so much in common.

Sax: He may as well be he's shit at everything.

Lucia: Is he dyslexic?

Sax: No.

Lucia: This one guy in class he's dyslexic, dyspraxic and bisexual. Elaina's dyslexic.

Elaina: Just because I'm dyslexic it doesn't mean I'm bisexual.

Lucia: What does he do?

Sax: Dropped out of Uni, pretends to play football. Goes to ASDA.

Lucia / Elaina: We love ASDA, You can shop and dance.

They start dancing and singing. Chris Brown: 'Loyal'

Sax:	Can you shut the fuck up. I was talking.
Elaina:	What?
Sax:	It's just the two of us now. – I'm stuck with him. I don't like it.

Elaina goes to Sax.

Elaina:	Not anymore. You got me. You've got your partner. Business partner.

She leans over to kiss him. Lucia pushes Elaina over.

Lucia:	Stop.
Elaina:	Get off me.
Lucia:	He has chicken juice all over his lips.
Elaina:	*(annoyed)* You fucking Twat.
Lucia:	Saved your life didn't I?
Elaina:	Babyface.
Lucia:	Sorry.
Sax:	Do you know what you want to be when you're older?
Elaina:	I want to be a/
Lucia:	Zoologist. She wants to be a zoologist.
Sax:	That's cool.
Elaina:	I guess I like animals.

Sax: I want to be a banker.

Lucia: Banker Wanker.

Sax: And what do you want to be?

Lucia: A student. I want to be a student.

Sax: *(to Lucia)* And after that?

Lucia: I dunno.

Elaina: It's getting dark.

Sax: Don't want to go home.

Elaina: Fuck going home. Let's go camping.

Get in the trolley -

Sax: Never been camping before.

Elaina: Well it's time you lost your camping virginity.

Exit – with a bit of Rule Britannia.

<u>'Ready or not here I come…'</u>

Tom enters on his bike.

Tom: *He chucks the bike down - trying to calm himself down.*

Sax – Sax - Count to ten. Calm down.

He's just a fucking kid. Deep breaths. I want to fucking kill him. 1 – 2 – 3 – 4 – 5 – 6 – 7 – 8 – 9 – 10 – deep breaths.

He picks up the bike again and goes.

<u>Scene 2. 'Paint Job'</u>

Josh enters wearing a painted suit. Anna is about to leave.

Josh: Wait.

Anna: What is that? I mean what is it?

Josh: My suit.

Anna: Unusual. Is it designer?

Josh: I designed it. Don't laugh.

Anna laughs.

Josh: Close your eyes and count to ten.

Anna: What again? *(she does it quickly)* 1-2-3-4-5-6-7-8-9-10

He repositioned himself.

Anna: It doesn't work —You look ridiculous. Like a floating head. What are you meant to be?

Josh: It's the perspective.

Anna: It's your face.

Josh: Here. Look. This artist does it. Look —

Anna: That's amazing.

Josh: And so I took these photos, I'm trying to get it just right so that the suit blends in with this tree.

He shows her the photos.

Anna: That's here.

Josh: Yes look.

Anna: Creative.

Josh: An experiment.

Anna: How long did it take you?

Josh: 22 and a half hours of photo taking.

Anna: Go and stand over there.

Josh: Here?

Anna: Yes. Just relax your arms. It's not bad but your face.

He holds a paint brush out to her. She shakes her head.

         Fuck no.

Josh: You could help.

Anna: No.

Josh: My face.

         I can do it myself. It's just – well I can do it. I'll do it myself. I'll just do it.

He attempts to do it but isn't good.

Anna: I've never painted anyone before.

Josh: Never nit combed anyone's hair before.

Anna: I'm not good – even the kids laugh at my drawings.

Josh: Go on.

She takes the brush.

Anna: Where do I start?

Josh: Anywhere.

Anna: I'll start with the nose.

Josh: Use the picture for reference.

She dips the brush in paint and puts it straight on his face.

Anna: There.

She starts painting him again.

Josh: Tickles.

Anna: Stop moving.

Josh: Yes. Sorry. Yes.

Anna: Today has been –

She steps back to look at her work

.

Josh: Odd.

Anna: Shh – stop talking.

(Josh signals a sorry)

When you said your suit was drying. I just thought maybe you had ketchup on it or something. But this – is. It's kind of relaxing, painting someone. Close your eyes.

When Tilly got her face painted it wouldn't come off for weeks. It was hilarious – poor thing looked like she had a skin disease.

Josh closes his eyes. Anna goes up close almost touching his lips with hers as she paints some more.

My parents think that Tilly, George and Ben are my housemates. *She laughs* Little do they know that: Tilly's six, George is three and Ben isn't even one. Should be a secret agent – you know – double life. Passport has expired, no one knows my address. Can't vote. Can't join the library. Haven't had an income for years, well as far as the government is concerned. Surprised no one thinks I'm dead. It's amazing really that I get away with it-

She steps close to him again and she gently blows air on to his lips.

There.

You can open your eyes.

Re-position yourself so I can't see you.

Josh is stood in his suit. Trying to be invisible.

Anna: Yes it's good. Hold your breath. And don't smile. Move an inch - to the left.

He moves.

Yes. That's good. Stop smiling.

Josh: (*Emerges again.*) I need to practice. It's like meditating. There's this man, he gets called Ice Man, he can control his body temperature, heart rate and breathing. He does it through meditation. Incredible. We forget what our bodies and minds are capable of. You know.

Anna: Yeah.

Josh: I want to feel what it's like to be invisible. Just vanish.

Anna: Just walk down the high-street.

Josh: In mathematical terms you can only become zero if you vanish. And zero remains undefined. 1 divided by zero remains un-changed. Zero takes no effect. In art it is often referred to as the vanishing point – the space between that no one understands. I want to know what it's like

– achieve that level – completely – free – to
be un-seen

Josh smells her neck.

Anna: What're you doing?

Josh: Smelling you.

Anna: It's getting dark.

Josh: Everyone has a smell.

Anna: I should go.

Josh: Wait.

Anna: It's getting late. Really late.

He smells again.

Josh: Everyone has a smell. Their own smell. You
smell of/

Anna: Sweat. It's hot, I've been running.

Josh: No. The whole time you've been painting
me. I couldn't smell a thing.

Anna: I don't put perfume on when I go jogging.

Josh: Smell me.

Anna: No.

Josh: I have this theory. Just smell me. Please.

Anna smells him.

So?

Anna: You don't smell of much just paint mostly.

Josh: Exactly.   My theory is when someone doesn't smell of anything. It means that people haven't let that person exist. You don't have a smell. You aren't loved. A baby smells wonderful. That's because babies are smothered with love. And you. It's true. Well I think it's true.   People don't notice people like us. Or they suddenly spot you but the first sense is smell. Do you ever feel like people don't see you and walk straight in to you? You said it yourself on the high-street.

Anna: Don't know what you're talking about.

Josh: You don't stay in their memory. A smell stays with people, people remember the smell of their grandparents. Stalkers take peoples clothes because smells can be captured.

Anna: I'm going.

Josh: I'm sorry. Was I rude?

Don't you ever just want to do it, disappear?

Josh touches her.

	You could, with me?
Anna:	Get off me. I don't know you. I know nothing about you. You're just a stranger.

Josh lets go.

Josh:	I'm sorry. *He goes to take his inhaler.*
Anna:	You know what I am loved and I have a life. I wanna keep it that way/
Josh:	I thought you-
Anna:	/Sometimes people think I'm flirting and I hope you didn't get the wrong end of the stick. But this is –I'm not doing it with you. I'm not doing anything with you? Okay? You understand?
Josh:	You'll like Brighton.
Anna:	I'm not going with you to Brighton.
Josh:	No I don't mean with me. Forget what I said. Please.
Anna:	Okay.
Josh:	Shall I comb your hair for a bit longer?
Anna:	No.
Josh:	Do you want any of this – this – maybe the Rolex?
Anna:	No. – No – No.

| Josh: | I'm sorry. Should never have spoken to you. It was just. I wasn't meant to talk – talk – just you know. You'll understand. I just – look after yourself, you are special. And so is everyone else, but you should feel it. |

Josh starts stepping away – 'vanishing'

> All the stuff you were saying. I just – thought maybe we had something in common.

| Anna: | All that I have in common with you is that I sat on this bench. |

Josh goes to his hiding place.

> Oh what? Is that it? Have you just vanished? Well thank god for that.

<u>Scene 3. *'Who judged first'*</u>

She stares for a while. Tom enters and Anna starts walking fast with the picture still in her bag on her back. Tom stops her.

Tom: Excuse me.

Anna starts to go in to a run.

Wait.

He blocks her.

Have you seen a kid hanging around?

Anna: Look. I'm busy.

Tom: Doing what? Talking to yourself?

Anna: Mind your own.

Tom: Sorry. You look nice. I need your help.

Anna: Great so you thought I looked nice. Do you think I smell nice too? You'll probably tell me I have a nice smile even though you haven't seen it. Or that I have nice hair, nice eyes. You want my number? Shall we just go into the bushes and get on with it? Or do you want me to take out my phone so you can just take it and run?

Tom: I don't want your number. Not my type, a bit old. No offence. Don't need your phone. Got one. But thanks, thanks for the offer, yeah. Listen my little brother's gone

96

missing. He's just a kid. So, if you see him can you tell him to come home? Probably pushing a trolley. Small. Brown eyes. Brown hair. It's getting dark. He shouldn't be out this late.

Anna: Sorry.

Tom: Sorry for what? Thinking that I was out to mug you, or fuck you? –

You shouldn't just judge people like that.

Tom exits leaving Anna stood there for a moment till she exits.

Scene 4. *'Our place, our den'*

Sax runs on he is holding a plastic bag and is exhilarated. The others emerge pushing the trolley that is full of stuff.

Elaina: Sax…

Sax has found the perfect place (climbing frame).

Sax: This is it.

Elaina: Home sweet home.

Elaina and Sax start building their camp. Lucia is using the bike pump to fan herself.

Elaina: Feels like we're at a festival.

Lucia: How do you know what it feels like, you've never been to one.

Elaina: Just imagine bands are playing – we are camping – and there's a load of overpriced hot dog stands and we've got wellies on – Glasto– Beyonce is about to go on with Dolly Parton and Jason Derulo

Lucia: Dolly Parton?

Elaina: Yeah – everyone's on stage – at the same time – About to do something fucking special. Are you alright, babyface?

Lucia: Don't be so patronising.

Sax has made the scarecrow. He steps back. At some point Josh has appeared. He is watching, he has carried the bag with him. He places it on the camp and steps back.

Elaina is admiring her work.

Sax: What do you think?

Lucia: What is it?

Elaina: Perfect.

Lucia: It's rubbish.

Elaina: Don't insult it.

Sax: He's our guardian angel.

Lucia: Creepy.

Elaina stands up and looks at the scarecrow.

Elaina: What shall we call him?

Sax: Paul.

Elaina: Paul?

Sax: Why not?

Elaina: Alright Paul.

Lucia: I don't like Paul.

Elaina: *(To Lucia)* What's your problem?

Sax: I could live here you know.

Lucia: This is stupid.

Lucia takes the KFC bucket off the scarecrow and stamps on it.

Sax: Hey.

Elaina: You killed Paul.

Sax: We can fix it.

Elaina: What's your problem? If you want to go – go home – just go. We don't need you. We built this. And what did you do? Nothing. Just sat there. Useless.

Lucia: So.

Elaina: If you want to go, go.

Lucia: Don't want to walk back alone.

Sax is still fixing.

Elaina: Leave it Sax.

He sits down and then gets up again to adjust something on the camp.

Now tell me – tell me what gives you the right to be the mood killer? I let you tag along. Join in. Why are you always like this?

Lucia: You owe me fifty quid.

Elaina: So.

Lucia:	You're waiting till I forget.
Sax:	When it gets dark the grass changes colour. Have you ever noticed that? Everything looks different.
Elaina:	I know how much I owe you.
Lucia:	Whatever.

Elaina lifts up her skirt slightly.

What's that?

Sax looks over. He gets up and walks away, lies on top of the trolley that is on its side. Staring up.

Elaina:	I do it with my compass in maths. Each line's a fiver.
Lucia:	You do that to yourself?
Elaina:	Yeah I cut myself.
Lucia:	And what do you do when you pay me back?
Elaina:	Stop picking at it.
Lucia:	Does it hurt?
Elaina:	A bit.
Lucia:	Just write it down.
Elaina:	This way I don't forget and get reminded a lot.

Lucia:	You shouldn't do that.
	Don't do it again. Please. – I don't like it.
Elaina:	Why do you care?
Lucia:	Cos you're my mate.
Elaina:	You won't tell anyone?
Lucia:	I'm your mate.
Sax:	Do you think we'll still do this when we're older?
Elaina:	Not drinking mouth-wash for the rest of my life.
Sax:	No, not like that. I mean hanging in the park.
Elaina:	Well yeah course. We should, the three of us put in our will that we want a bench in the park. In memory of us. So we can come here even when we're dead.

Sax spots the bag.

Sax:	What is this?
Lucia:	What?
Sax:	This bag.

He goes up to get it. Elaina takes it from him and un-zips it.

Elaina:	Loads of stuff in here.

Sax: Probably belongs to some homeless guy.

Lucia holds up a watch.

Lucia: Look.

Elaina: Is that a Rolex?

Lucia: Got to be a fake right?

Sax: Let's see. *He examines it.* Looks genuine.

Elaina: Go on try it on. Not many kids can say that
                  they've worn a Rolex.

Sax: I'm not a kid.

Elaina: Go on.

Sax: Alright.

Elaina: You look like a proper banker now -
                  Someone could cut your hand off for that.

*Sax takes it and puts it on. The girls carry on looking at the
stuff.*

Lucia: Maybe someone nicked it dumped it.
                  There's an old iphone in here.

Elaina takes the bag and the phone.

Elaina: You need a phone.

Sax: What if it's some kind of trap. Some kind of
                  set up and now our fingerprints will be all
                  over this shit/

Lucia: Maybe someone got attacked.

Sax is wearing the watch.

                What if. What if, it's hers – did you hear about that woman. She got raped, murdered in the park – this could be her bag.

                Creepy.

Elaina: It's a man's watch. So it can't be hers.

Elaina is setting the timer on her phone.

Lucia: Maybe he's still out there – crazy rape murderer. And those are the clothes and things he killed her in.

Elaina: Maybe she rejected him. And he felt so alone. So sad. He can't live without her. Hung himself, cut himself, taken loads of pills and that, this is all his stuff he stripped off and his body is somewhere naked with a broken heart.

Elaina holds the phone up. She drops it into the bag but keeps the bag on her lap.

                That would make this a dead man's phone.

Sax: You're freaking me out.

Lucia: This is dark – really dark.

Elaina: I mean if he could see us now. With all his stuff treating it like this. I mean what would he do? What would he say? Would he kill us?

The phone in the bag rings and Elaina drops the bag and kicks it towards Sax.

Sax: Fuck.

Lucia: What do we do?

Elaina: Pick it up.

Sax: No way.

They stare at the bag.

Lucia: The dead man's phone.

Sax: What if there's some angry guy looking for it. Ready to beat the crap out of us. Right now it looks like we nicked it.

Elaina: Sax, pick it up.

Sax: Nah, I'm not touching it.

Elaina: Maybe it's his ghost wants to communicate with us. I want to know what he has to say. *(She picks it up)* Hello.

Elaina listens and screams and bursts into laughter.

Lucia: What's so funny?

Elaina: You fell for it. I made my phone ring.

See what I did was put my phone in the bag on a timer. And the timer went off so it sounded like it was ringing.

Lucia sees Josh.

Lucia: Oh Fuck.

Elaina: Are you trying to be funny?

Lucia: No, There's someone there?

Elaina: Ha ha very funny. If it's your mate Jesus just tell him to piss off.

Lucia: No really there's someone there–

Elaina and Sax finally see him and jump.

Sax: Fucking hell.

Lucia: How long has he been there?

Sax: Shit.

Lucia: What the fuck is he wearing?

Elaina: *(shouts)* What you looking at, Freak?

Piss off.

Sax: Probably wants his stuff back.

Elaina: *(Towards Josh)* This your stuff?

Lucia: *(Towards Josh)* Fuck off!

Sax: Can we just go.

Lucia:	How long has he been standing there?
Sax:	Lets get out of here.
Elaina:	No.
Lucia:	I don't like him. Lets go.
Elaina:	No. We aren't going nowhere.
Lucia:	Can't stay here with him – watching.
Elaina:	We were here first.
	This is our camp.

She throws the bag at him.

	Is this what you're after?
Lucia:	Did he just close his eyes?
Elaina:	*(to Josh)* You here to scare us?
	What you want?
Lucia:	He's creepy.
Sax:	Is he breathing?
Lucia:	What's he wearing?
Elaina:	Some kind of camouflage. What? *(To Josh)* Wanted to sneak up on us. Flash us? Wanka.
	You scared us. You scared my friend.

Lucia:	*(To Josh)* What do you want? Pedo. Wanka.
Elaina:	How much?
Lucia:	What?
Elaina:	If I touch him. How many points?
Sax:	Not playing.
Elaina:	What are the rules?
Sax:	This isn't a game.
Elaina:	Life's a game isn't that right Lucia?
Lucia:	Yeah, life's a game and I need to play it.
Elaina:	And?
Lucia:	We set the rules and other people obey it.
Elaina:	Good girl. So the rules?
Lucia:	The rules are. Erm – You have to touch him. Touch his face, for that you'll get ten points. So you can deduct a tenner off what you owe me.

Elaina does it – She steps forward. Elaina touches Josh. Elaina jumps back, screams and laughs.

Elaina:	Fuck – right. Your turn next. For one hundred – thousand gazillion points touch his cock. Yeah. Go on.

108

Lucia steps forward.

>Wait. Take the Swiss army for protection.

Lucia takes the knife.

Lucia: I don't need protection.

Lucia goes, she looks at him. Josh moves and she cuts him.

Elaina: You cut him you fucking cut him.

Elaina drags Josh forward and to the ground.

Elaina: Fucking. Pedo. WANKA.

Lucia gets closer.

Lucia: Pedo.

Elaina: Fucking Pedo.

Elaina and Lucia push him forward into the circle.

Lucia: Yeah Pedo.

Elaina: Creep. Fucker – dogger – flasher.

Lucia: Sax. Go on.

Elaina: Right. Your turn Sax.

Sax: Nah.

Elaina: Yeah. Go on Sax. I'll give you thirty points if you – cut his nipple off.

Elaina and Lucia giggle. They surround Josh.

Sax: Don't need points. And I'm not touching anyone's nipple.

Elaina: Alright – alright – mark him – cut him –

Lucia: Carve him

Elaina: Come on. This look normal to you? Look at him. He's asking for it.

Sax: I can't.

Elaina: Right. I'll give you one hundred fucking points.

Sax: Don't need points. Don't care about the points.

Elaina: Aright, fifty quid.

Sax: Fifty quid? One cut fifty quid?

Shows him the fifty. Sax goes over to take it.

Elaina: Oh no – no – not until you've done it – go on.

Sax: Fuck – alright – one cut – one cut fifty quid.

He does it. Elaina starts filming.

Sax: Shit –

Elaina claps as she is filming. Josh screams. Sax sees Elaina filming.

                    What you doing – don't film me.

Stop filming. This could get us in to shit. Fuck. Stop.

Give me the money.

Elaina: What money?

Sax: The Fifty Quid.

Elaina: Don't know what you're talking about.

Sax: You said

Lucia: You need to do it again.

Sax: I fucking did it – turn that off.

You need to give me the fifty quid. I hurt him. You said.

Josh gets up and goes.

Elaina: Go on then. Fuck off

Lucia: Fuck off.

Elaina: Do your walk of shame. Pedo.

Lucia: Pedo.

Sax: You lied.

Elaina: I didn't lie. You didn't do it properly.

Sax: He needs help. Call an ambulance.

Lucia: He deserved it.

Elaina:	We aren't calling anyone.
Sax:	Give me your phone.
Elaina:	Fuck off.
	You aren't having it.
Sax:	We need to call an ambulance. We shouldn't have done that.
Elaina:	I didn't cut him – you both did.
Lucia:	No way – You can't say that.
Elaina:	I didn't do anything. But what you did was fucking brave.
Lucia:	But –
Elaina:	I'm proud of you. It took fucking guts.
Lucia:	What if/
Elaina:	What if no what ifs. You both aren't gonna tell anyone about this. Not a word. Nothing. Okay? He deserved it. And I've got a picture – if you do anything I'll social media the crap out of it. If you say anything.
Sax:	Give me your phone.
Elaina:	What if I show the picture to your brother?
Sax:	You fucking dare.

112

Elaina: Swear your silence.

Elaina looks to Lucia.

Lucia: I swear.

Sax goes to grab her phone.

Elaina: Get off me.

Sax: Give it here. You made me do that.

Elaina: Back off.

     Get off me Sax. Right. Fuck you.

She screams

     Rape – Rape – Rape.

Lucia joins in.

Sax lets go of her.

     Back off –

Sax: Give me your phone.

He gets closer.

Elaina: *(shouts)* Rape.

Sax: Stop it.

Lucia: Leave us alone weirdo.

Sax: I'll tell – I'll tell on you.

Elaina: Got a picture where you're the only one doing it – alright – think about that – Think about that – loser, probably got a spotty sweaty smelly little dick.

Sax: We should give him his stuff back.

Elaina: There is no we.

Lucia takes Elaina's hand. Pause.

Fuck you.

(*To Lucia*) Lets go home

They exit.

Sax: Don't leave me. Please.

Sax stands and echoes his brothers greeting: 'If Zombies attack'. Sax takes the bag and sits in front of the Den organising, trying to clean the knife.

Scene 5 *'When Zombies attack'.*

Tom enters. Sax jumps up drops the knife and wraps his arms round him.

Tom: Get off me.

Sax: I want to go home.

Tom: Been looking for you. What you been doing?

Sax: Nothing.

Tom: Nothing?

Sax: I want to go home. Tired.

Tom: You've got some explaining to do.

Sax: Did you see us? Did you see anything? It's just - A lot has happened. And I well – these girls – and – this man, did you see him – the grass was turning blue– this painted man – His suit – His face – I dunno – it was creepy all painted and he was smiling – and the red against the paint from his blood – it was – I didn't want to- but he looked sad – the paint all over him – and he –

Tom looks at him and then looks at his eyes.

Tom: You're on drugs aren't you?

Sax: No.

Tom: Who would give a fourteen year old drugs?

Sax: No –

He takes the bag and empties his bag.

Tom: And what's this?

             I knew it –

He looks around. Tom walks around the den.

             This where you keep all your stolen shit?

Sax: No we found it. And some people gave us stuff.

Tom: You were always good at building dens weren't you?

Sax: Yeah.

Tom empties the plastic bag he's been carrying of coins.

Tom: Found these.

Sax: Shouldn't be touching my stuff.

Tom: Each bag's a pound right?

             You listening?

             Sax?

             Each bag's a pound right?

Sax: Yes, each bag's one pound.

116

Tom: Where did you get them?

Sax: You chuck em in the bin.

Tom: Yeah but there's just so many of them. So many coins.

Sax: I collect money. Alright. You know that. You've seen me. That's what I do.

Tom: Sofa was lined, riddled.

Sax: I collect at least 50p in coppers a day.

Tom: This isn't just 50p. I'm talking hundreds of pounds.

Sax: If I make 50p, then in a year I'd make around 182 pounds. And lets say I've been doing that for 7 years. And then I get a bit extra here and there.

Tom: I'm not stupid.

Sax: I could easily make well, 1,872 pounds.

Tom: How much?

Sax: You know I collect money. I collect coins. You chuck em in the bin so I take them, that's how it all started. Sometimes I find it. Most people will just give it to you. And I. I protect it. I'm keeping our money safe because the banks can't. And you're not good with money. I'm trying to protect it. You're not good with money.

Tom: *(he pushes Sax hard)* You little shit. Do you wanna know who's been banging at our door? And all this time – you've been stealing. Bet that's where my tenner went.

Sax: I want to go home.

Tom: Sax. Those two guys banging on our door. They're what we call bailiffs. And they want everything. We've run out – run out of money – I don't have a student allowance anymore – you think I like signing on – they found out I dropped out – Came back to all this shit-

Sax: I thought –

Tom: My job is to look after you.

Sax: I don't need looking after.

Tom: You're fourteen.

Sax: You should have told me.

Tom: These guys keep coming. Knocking. I decide to sell mum's jewellery. There's nothing of value, well that's what I thought. But all this time I am sitting on it. Bag after bag of money.

	Stuffed like drugs in a cuddly toy. All this time – made me feel so stupid. There's me looking for anything I could find.
Sax:	I'm keeping it safe.
Tom:	And I start counting. Counting your money. Our money. The stolen money.
Sax:	You won't understand.
Tom:	Try me.
Sax:	I'm keeping it safe.

Tom grabs Sax.

Tom:	Where did you get it…?
Sax:	I er-
Tom:	I'm listening.

Sax:	Well. – I find it. – the money –/
Tom:	You nick it –
Sax:	…and when I get £10 in the shape of a note. I change it in to pennies. – So – Suddenly it loses value in your eyes, you don't want it. You don't like it. Those manky brown coins that make your hands sweat and smell of metal. The effort of counting it all up. – I've made it easy – all the bags are worth a

119

pound each. Right? Nice and simple. But no – no one really wants these. Even the bank isn't keen on it. And that's the point. These are bags of gold and it's safer than paper cos paper burns. What do archaeologists find: old coins they don't find any paper money unless it's preserved in one of those special tubes with papyrus in it. Do you get it? This is safe. Only kids or weirdos care about pennies...

Tom: What you going to do with it?

Tom hits him. Sax gets up.

Sax: ...I'm clever with money – you're not. Remember – I like monopoly you hate it you burnt it. You aren't good with money. And – well – You know what. When the shop keepers see these pennies they shake their heads and pretty much give me the chocolate or whatever it is, for free because they can't be arsed to count it... I'm keeping it safe.

Tom: The whole place lined with your filth. Your shit everywhere./

Sax: /My shit – Eventually I'll be able to turn all this shit in to bigger things. Maybe a house. Maybe a car. Maybe a holiday. I make it look worthless to you so you don't really want it. You don't really want the hassle of managing your money. You don't want to have to count it. You prefer the card. I make it easy for you. You wait. You'll see I'll be the richest kid. I am going to be a banker in a nice clean suit with silver cuffs and lots of aftershave and bright white teeth. I'll be going on holidays to Egypt swimming with dolphins and I'll head to Brazil and meet some girls. And all the girls will have Brazilians there, and that's good right? And then I'll get in to golf, maybe I'll wear colourful socks with my slick suit and have a diamond rimmed iphone and a gold tooth. Right here. You'll never be rich. You'll see I'm on the Fast Track out of here. And all you do is buy coco-pops. I don't even like coco-pops /*(cross over)*

Tom: You told me you liked them, that's why I buy them./

Sax: /I can look after myself./

Tom: /I searched the flat/

Sax: /I don't need you. I didn't want you to come back. I don't even like you/

Tom: /Tore the place up. And then. It starts raining money – I look up – the ceiling. Bang/

Sax: /You're a loser/

Tom: /Could have killed me. All that crap. Crashing down. Magpie. Fucking magpie. Our flat collapsed. Caved in on itself. The weight – of your obsession. I could have died. Sax. I could have died. Without knowing what a freak you are-/

Sax /If zombies attack we will fight… when we sink into the ocean we will swim… before time there was man and before man there were two brothers./

Tom: /I'm done Sax./

Sax stands watching. Tom turns around and looks at him. Sax stays looking he does the greeting silently (zombies attack…)

/I'm going to close my eyes and count to ten then I want you gone. Vanished, out of my life.

1 – 2 – 3 – 4 –

5 – 6 – 7 –

Sax takes the bag of coins (as much as he can) and exits.

8 – 9 – 10 –

Tom opens his eyes and picks up some coins off the ground. He goes to the den and sits and picks up coins and starts counting continuously to 10 – the count to ten underscoring the next scenes)

Epilogue:

'To be nothing'

At the bench. Josh sits.

Josh: To be nothing. In mathematical terms is to be zero. And to be zero you have to vanish. But to vanish you need to cease to exist. There are different ways of doing it. Attempting it. *He looks up. He strokes his forehead.* You can control pain. Vanish mentally. Bodies – become objects, and an object becomes projected on. The object will always be there. In some formation. Start and end as dust. But it's still dust – and it can enter someone else's lungs. Corpses smell. But not a good smell. An odour, a type of gas is produced. A human can not detect or smell the odour of a body under water. Water. Like an inhaler. Inhale and hold your breath till the stuff fills your lungs.

He takes a deep breath.

'I met a man who wasn't there...'

Anna enters, she inhales and looks around. She is wearing different clothes (a new day).

Anna: 1,200 people run in this park? And I was the one that sat on this bench.

She sits on the bench. And Josh stands in his vanishing point.

Josh?

I er- well – I got it – The note on the back – on the back of Nick Drake. I hope the experiment is – working – I'm sorry – I er – what I should have said is, don't – A house. A house in Brighton. I can't accept it. You can't just give someone a house. Are you there?

I had an idea. Tell me if you like it and if you don't why don't you tell me. Tell me. It's simple. A bit crazy – I'll - look after it, live in it. Until you come back. And I want to invite other people to join me.

UNDERSCORE: Tom counting 1-10 and Josh counting 10-0.

I google earthed it and it looks big. So I want other people to live in it. I think I'll call it: The big house warm up. I need to work on - on the name. But the idea is that people can live in it as long as they love it.

And – well – I'm excited about it. I think it
could work. And I think – well I think it
will smell and sound wonderful - people
cooking, talking. And it's close to the sea.
And – well I thought you'd like it.

I liked talking to you.

She smiles.

I don't know what to say, really but
thanks.

She turns around.

If I close my eyes and count to ten will you-

$1 - 2 - 3 - 4 - 5 - 6 - 7 - 8 - 9 - 10$

*All characters emerge and start counting to ten and running.
Josh is standing (counting backwards) Anna is still standing
and counting. Tom is back in the flat counting coins and
putting them in to tens. And Elaina and Lucia and Sax run
round the audience counting to ten at different times.
Crescendos with music.*

Elaina: *(is heard)* $8 - 9 - 10 - $ GO!

Blackout.

END.